Finding Closure

Dedication

This book is dedicated to anyone on their journey towards moving on from the past.

With time, you will heal. With time, you will continue to grow.

Contents

Chapter One:
Her

Jessica Burgos

he was my dream come true,
but we woke up too soon.
he'll always be a part of my story,
even after our love ends in June.

Finding Closure

we had an Autumn love,
with the breeze pushing us closer together,
falling into each other,
wrapped around each other,
until we were stuck together
for what felt like forever.

Jessica Burgos

let my love stick to you like vaseline,
an addiction that won't come clean,
it's okay if you get stuck to me.
don't stop me now, i'm your living queen,
cherry lipstick on your cheek,
let your friends see,
kiss me and fill my lungs, help me breathe,
these nights never end and
we will keep reliving our fun
until we meet again.

Finding Closure

we fell in love under the stars
and even in the nighttime,
they were some of my brightest days.

you satisfied all five love languages,
and i craved you in all senses.

the months i've known you
have felt more like a lifetime,
like maybe heaven exists
and it's our eternal peace.

Jessica Burgos

i loved watching you fall for me,
because i didn't know i could ever mean
so much to someone.

the honeymoon phase is always the easiest,
because first impressions feel like they'd
last.
time is the slowest
while our identities are masked.
honeymoon is fun,
she gives us a new perspective on love.
honeymoon is a teacher,
she instructs us to release our past hurt and
fear.
honeymoon is convincing,
she persuades us to accept new love as
familiar, rather than foreign.

she convinces us that this love is forever.

i don't know why i always speak of cotton
candy skies
when i fall for your brown eyes.
as i prefer a nighttime sky
over a pink sunset horizon line,
because i can't make eye contact with the
sun
but i can admire a beaming moon miles
away and call it Love
and just like the moon never needed stars
around it to shine,
you glow on your own just fine.

i don't know why i always speak of cotton
candy skies
when i fall for your brown eyes.
as i prefer a nighttime sky
and it's mystery, curiosity, charm, and
elegance.

i don't know why everyone always speaks
of shades of pink in a sunrise
but forgets the moon is still there glistening.
he gets lonely sometimes
but he's still there listening.

i lost interest in cotton candy skies
ever since i fell for your brown eyes.

no, i wasn't on cloud nine with you,
we were on the moon.
the sky was easy to reach
so we aimed for the stars,
but we laughed
because they don't shine like we do.
and when the sun rose everyday
it kissed us good morning,
and told me that you were
all the warmth i needed
and that you were my blessing.

no, i wasn't on cloud nine with you,
we walked on rocks.
the universe always found a way
to keep us together when life got hard.
and when life got hard,
the Earth rained to cry
and we got sad but you held me
in your arms,
leaving all the pain behind,
leaving all the rain outside.

no, we weren't perfect
but at least i had you by
my side.

Jessica Burgos

i once saw a world that was hard enough
to put me at demise
and you showed me that my time here
doesn't have to be
full of cycles of
cries and goodbyes.
you taught me how to love life
in such a short amount of time.

you put your head in my lap
and a weight gets lifted off of my shoulders.

Jessica Burgos

i just want to thank you
for the beginning of this relationship
and thank you a little less for the rest,
because your good behavior withered
through the seasons.

the honeymoon phase was the most gentle,
the best,
and i will kiss it goodbye because i know
i'll never feel that with you again.

Jessica Burgos

we were sweeping our problems under the
rug hoping we can simply step over them.

but it only made the trash thicker
and the dust grayer.

now look at all of the dirt we have collected.
now look at the mess we have made.

our problems didn't just come up,
they slept with us every night.
they showed up in our faces
and they went from being complicated
to complex
to casual.
we pretended that our problems were
normal.

you were only my first best
and i told you that after the first time
i just couldn't stop thinking about the sex.
and you told me that was okay,
but what is okay about an addiction, a
craving over someone i feel like i just met.

what happens at night when the water turns
to wine
and the glass can't glisten in the sunshine,
as the bed swallows us
and squeezes the secrets out of us,
but we ignore the truths about each other
for the sake of making love together
and pretending like we make sense,
pretending like we matter.

Jessica Burgos

i am bleeding from the inside out,
with red rivers overflowing the kitchen floors.
you notice
and you squeeze out every bit of me until i'm
dry
knowing that you can take every part of me
and knowing that i will let you.

i need to differentiate between good sex and intimacy. because with you, they were never the same.

Jessica Burgos

overthinking makes my heart ache,
but i get a sweet tooth when i kiss you.
nauseous, i guess i'm love sick
and sick of love.

nothing lasts forever,
you and i both knew that.
but we were dumb enough to think that
our love was the exception.

Jessica Burgos

our love was the apple of our eye,
red and ripe,
sweet and fulfilling,
until it wasn't satisfying us anymore.
we gave each other the fruit of our labor
and we play with it and
drop it on the ground.
then, our love is no longer red but it is
brown and bruised,
it is too late to eat,
it is too late to cherish,
as it has already gone bad and
we must throw it away,
we must let it perish.

the breakup was hard
but learning to live with myself was even
harder.
because time was too slow in healing me
and anxiety was my biggest disturber.

the breakup
was a process that felt less like a
transformation
and more of a challenge,
i felt like i was given more than i could
handle.

the healing process did not feel like growth
but felt more like i was withering.

Jessica Burgos

and when i see the bright light peaking
through my window, shining on my face,
i remember that i haven't been outside in days.

Finding Closure

it takes me 10 minutes to cry
but it takes me 4 hours to understand why, i
think it helps me leave my past behind
or at least that's what i tell myself after the
3rd time of crying this week.

Jessica Burgos

the shower water burns my skin but i like it,
it is more comforting than the lakes and the
oceans.

crimson lipstick, stained teeth,
but the shower wipes the smile from my
cheeks.

this is my altar, this is where i let myself go,
this is the place i feel most at home.

Finding Closure

i try to use sleep to forget about you
but you find a way to be in my dreams
anyway.

38

i want to go with the flow but its tossing me
around and moving me too fast.

i feel restless, i feel stiff,
i feel how hard it is to breathe and i choke on
my spit
until it builds up like an ocean
and my mind becomes a reckless ship.

these blue walls that were once keeping me
alive are now eating away at me
and my anxiety inside.

you can't just speak like that to someone you
love.

you told me that love was the foundation
but our stability was lacking
and love on its own was never enough to
save us.

Jessica Burgos

did your lack of trust in me create
boundaries
where you put up a wall to be separated
from me?

i didn't just ask for more communication,
i asked for more cooperation.

Jessica Burgos

i knew we were over
when the silence in the room
was split into two,
when the silence in the room
felt uncomfortable
while sitting next to you.

it was so easy for you to listen
but it was even easier for you to forget.
my concerns became your concerns too
but only for a moment.

Jessica Burgos

i wish you were still the man
that you were in the beginning.

how can a person who was once my safe
space become my broken place?

you grew thorns from your belly
and i could feel the pain of your past
every time i hugged you.
i don't blame you.
but i wish you did not let your past define
you.

i ask myself,
were you changing into a different person
or were you revealing who you always
were?

Jessica Burgos

i wanted to reach the moon
and i still do
but because you had a fear of heights
i limited my comfort zone for you.

you grew a habit of talking over me
and i think you started to enjoy making me
feel small.

Jessica Burgos

i should have spoken up when you spoke
down on me
i should have spoken up when you didn't
let me speak.

i lost all autonomy.

i didn't have to look in the mirror
to see who i was
and who i was becoming.
i just had to look at you.

you hid behind a wall of your insecurities
but you didn't realize that these walls
surrounded
me too.

i understand you losing faith in me
but i don't understand
keeping me on a leash
like i'm your property.

i had secrets too
but at least i shared mine with you.

Finding Closure

my nails went from tearing into your back
to ripping the hair out of my head
to pulling the memories out of our bed
to struggling to hold onto what we had left.

Jessica Burgos

i'll only say sorry when i have to
and watch you cry when you want to
because i see your pain
and it doesn't move me.
i believe you deserve cruelty
and the same treatment you handed me,
a love story without the beauty.

the moment i left you was the loneliest moment
of my life.

Jessica Burgos

thick skin only lasts so long.
when i tear at the first sound of our song,
hearing the first notes only to remind me
of the ringing of your phone call
and picking it up, not expecting your words
to be an open wound with salt,
leaving me breathless, yet fully aware of
what i have gotten myself into.

my mind can't stop racing.
it goes something like this,
"how can i be more like this
how can you be more like this
how can we be more like us
are you really the one
is it love or is it lust
how did i lose your trust
how long have i been up
for me to ask if we are each other's anomaly
were we written in the stars or is it false
astrology
why couldn't i find your honesty
how could we bond through music but have
not found our harmony
how can my brain find peace in curiosity
when every night i get sleepy and wake up
at 3 am
realizing that between us
we are the ultimate dichotomy?"

i was healing
but i wasn't my own healer -
you were,
the thing to stitch me back together.
i went from being ripped up pieces of paper
to being a whole love letter.

but the problem was you were my writer
and that without you, i had no creator.

i heard my intuition speak to me.
her telling me that it is not too late to
walk away,
that i can finally be free,
that starting my new life was only a door
step away.
but i silenced her
and told her,
"let me stay one more day.
let me make sure this is the place i want to
stay
and that this is the house i want to call home
and that this relationship is the right
foundation we have built upon."
but of course, this only lasted for some time,
as 405 days have already passed
and i wish i could go back
to tell my intuition
that i should have listened to her the first
time.

i want to get back all of the control you took
away from me.

if i like me,
who else do i need!
not the garbage man i carry with me
everyday,
giving me baggage
when i'm just learning how to get rid of my
own trash.

every night i light a candle
and fall in love with the flame
and the way the wax cannot handle
the heat of the fire that stands high and
grounded.

every night i light a candle
and fall in love with the flame
because it reminds me of my anger
and rage that no one around me can handle.

every night i light a candle
and fall in love with the flame
and imagine silencing the world with my anger
and melt everyone like wax
and be the only one left standing and
grounded.

Finding Closure

with you,
i did not have to create a facade
and that was the scariest part.
i was watching myself be vulnerable
and i didn't do anything to stop it.

68

much like the sun,
i stand alone.
i feel unrecognizably beautiful
yet often forgotten about when i'm in the
room.

i was afraid to admit
that i had flaws too
and i was afraid to admit
that maybe they stuck with you.

i thought i loved myself
but i guess not enough to
stop settling for you.

let it be known that we are both victims to
each other.

my mother is a complex and complicated
woman.
i have observed her flawed ways.

my mother is a complex and complicated
woman.
she taught me
emotional intelligence
but only how to not practice it.
she taught me crying when i don't get my
way, leave it to her to mix
insecurities with stressful
tendencies.

she taught me
that i do not want to
be like her
anymore.

Finding Closure

i learned to enjoy crying
because it feels like i'm cleansing,
the pain leaks and
the tears kiss my cheeks
gently reminding me
it is time for my body to be
at peace
again.

Jessica Burgos

what i want is external validation
but what i need is internal love.

Finding Closure

i wish i said
the words i never said
but we have grown apart now
and i cannot bring to life what is already
dead
with the thoughts that have been stuck in
my head.

Jessica Burgos

we wanted to travel the world together
and now i have to imagine living life
without you.

i reflect on the memories,
the good and the bad,
but i know i must kiss them goodbye,
even though i want to revisit them
one more time.

the road we have drove down
has now split into two.
i am now learning how to look back at you
and continue to move.

Finding Closure

i am still learning what it's like to be on my
own,
and i feel so alone.
but i know i will be better off without you.

if i can live before you, then i will live after
you.

Finding Closure

i wanted closure
but i know it won't be coming from you
because no matter how many texts i send
to see you again
it will only hurt me more
and the memories will still be there after.

i wanted closure
but i know it won't be coming from you
because no matter how much i pretend
that i don't have love for you
i can't change how i feel
until i give myself the time to heal.

i reflect on what i have learned from you:

i should've validated your feelings the way you
validated mine.
i should've set boundaries and verbalized what
they were.
i should've been more present with you instead
of pretending like i was.
i should've communicated that i was falling out
of love instead of keeping it a secret.
and now, i should find closure in the way i
loved and hurt and learned.

i'm getting closer to the closure i need from
you,
but i'm getting it from inside me.
i'm not there yet, but i know i will be.

we ended in summer
and now we must blossom without each
other.

Chapter Two:
Him

she was bittersweet
but her love didn't stick.
she'll always be a part of my story,
even after our love ends in June.

we had an Autumn love,
watching the leaves fall with us
as we fell for each other.

and as we grew with the seasons,
we knew that our time together
went by too soon.

you are so warm and sweet
your hugs are all i need.
honey is what you call me
when you miss me
and you can't get enough of me and see
that when we collide we make a
beautiful mixture
and i crave you on nights
we don't sleep together.
but when we do, i stick to your
body because it's hard to let go of
in the morning.
you're relaxing.
i have a sweet tooth
for the love you give me
and i never want to get rid of it.

Finding Closure

i was tied up in your arms
watching the world stop,
closing in on your thoughts
about our love being your favorite art
and our feelings growing like a boiling pot,
i watched myself fall into your heart
and let myself get caught.

Jessica Burgos

you made brown my favorite color,
i now remember the details of your eyes
for the sake of dreaming about them later.

kissing your lips was the parting of the red sea,
deep, and nothing i've ever seen,
it's a miracle just to feel this holy,
with you gushing out your love for me
i'm put under your spell.
minutes feel like hours,
only when you have that much power
over me.

raspberry is sweet and satisfies my teeth,
stains and leaves a beautiful mess we create.
each time we lay together, candy sticks
and i become a sugar addict
and a little love sick.

i touch the petals in your garden flowers
waiting for them to swallow me whole,
because your lips are the entrance
while your body is a chamber i explore.
you give me access,
you give me acceptance
to everything you are and how we bleed
together.

your eyes look like the sun
but mostly when they are closed,
eyelashes creating beams
shining above your nose,
you are simply enchanting
and i just love admiring you glow.

Finding Closure

let me be the place you come home to.
where you find good news
and where you lie to feel brand new,
a safe haven of solace and gratitude
filled with your favorite comfort food.

you'll never want to lose me,
the place you want to come home to.

i discovered the feeling of butterflies when i fell
for you and now i let these wings guide me to
you.

i am not safe in my bed,
but i am safer in your neck
where my head is buried like a hole,
and a spot saved for me in heaven.

your aroma soothes me
while i melt into your skin
and for the first time i feel complete,
not a fragment that once was, but a piece of
forever ahead.

i made it to 24th street
to find you sitting on the east wing
where drinks are cold
and bodies are hot.
this is where love meets lust
and i confused the two when i saw you.
i took a shot
at bringing you into my life
and you stayed with me for a couple years
but left me not much longer after that.
now the start of us
lives and dies on 24th street
and the street stays bleak to me.

a warm shower feels like a good hug
when all i wanted from you was some sweet
love.
i let tears run down my cheek
because i hoped that you would dry them for
me.
we move in together
and i paint the living room walls blue
so that maybe my anxiety doesn't take over
at least one room.
i write rants about you till my hand cramps
but at least the paper doesn't stop listening to
me.
i ignore my laundry next to our door
because i feel too comfortable having a to do list
and i like being busy and away from you.
i look at our old photographs
and see how happy we were
in hopes that tomorrow will be better.

and i'll end up hoping again tomorrow too.

i saw the fire rise between us
and i saw you extinguish it.

hey, it's me
i didn't know you got up from bed
until i woke up at 6 am
and noticed you had left.
your hair tie and chapstick,
i just found it,
i didn't think it was something you'd miss.
but please call me back and let me know when
you'll stop by.
i'll make us coffee or tea, whatever you like
my love,
just give me a chance to say goodbye.

i felt you falling out of love with me months
before we ended.

Finding Closure

i knew we were over when we made love but
not passion
and the foreplay was great but the climax was
lacking,

because you were filled with me
but i was filled with nothing,

and while i kept feeling empty inside of you,
i let you partake in my body as if i still meant
something to you.

we were like the youth,
finding open slots in our schedule to see each
other for half an hour,
gossiping to our friends after each encounter,
bringing you fresh flowers
and watching you keep them only to wither
away silently on top of your dresser,
and then taking out our journals to write about
all the drama and problems we had together.

waves carried my body to a calm shore
then you took control of the sea.
things became restless
and since then, i haven't found peace.

you found my weakest spots
and made them your own,
taking every chance you had to sew
my insecurities into blankets
to cover up the many that you had.

you weren't loving me for who i really was,
you were trying to change me into who you
wanted me to be.

it was easy for you
to forget to be gentle with me when things got
hard.
your love deteriorated as our bombs went off.

after a while, i started to feel like i was chasing you,
to get you to love me the way that you used to.

slow down, you're moving on too fast.

it is exhausting to speak
when you don't believe me,
placing dirt on my name
and wiping it on my face,
claiming that i don't love you
and that i love someone else,
when i never loved someone
as best as i loved you.

all you ever did was create chaos in the silence.

i continue to follow this path
of confusion and doubt with you,
hoping to find the love we lose
every few months from being out of touch
with who we were in the beginning,
feeling like eternity of affection is far away.
but this road is lone and long and deserted
and i'm starting to realize that i'll never reach
the end of the road
in which i can achieve happiness with you.

what happens when the glass breaks,
and what once was a stable space becomes a
table that shakes,
and we find out that our foundation of love is
actually built upon hate.

i never knew i had a friend and an enemy until
i met sleep.
she's where i want to be to forget about you
and me,
but i still can't escape you
since i sometimes still dream of you and me.

i know i shouldn't go back to who hurt me, but
i'm so tempted to because it feels good being
somewhere i'm comfortable.

i can't stop checking my phone,
waiting for attention from you
because i'm trying so hard to avoid
being by myself and being alone.

Jessica Burgos

i'm tossing and turning
because it's hard not having you.
i breathe but it's not helping my anxiety
and i'd text you but it won't help my sobriety.
so i'd rather stay quiet, shut down, and die a
little inside
and check my phone 95 times a day in hopes
that you'll think of me in your timeline.

i keep holding onto hope but hope wants to let go of me.

i cry because i know no amount of love i give
would have fixed us
if you don't feel the same way anymore.

i didn't know i could cry this much,
and i never thought you'd be the reason.

you treat me so cruel,
i'm hoping for someone to take me away from
you
because i know you won't be helping me
or treating me
or loving me better
anytime soon.

we painted our walls blue
in hopes that it would give us peace
but blue is still blue
and blue is still dreary
and blue is still bleak to me.

i feel like i'm your favorite victim.

Finding Closure

and even with your flaws
and how much you hurt me,
i feel like i didn't deserve a woman like you.

128

and even with my flaws
i thought i was so good to you,
but looking back i know that's not true.

i feel like i became your baggage.

Jessica Burgos

your voice cracks when you yell at me
but i can't help but hear dry roads
and exhausted droughts
of someone that hasn't been loved right in so
long.

i'm so sorry i could not quench your thirst.

i was hearing you but i wasn't listening,
just waiting till i could speak over you.

Jessica Burgos

i raised my voice at you
as if i was afraid you would steal mine.

i dominated every room,
i controlled every conversation,
and you waited patiently for your contribution.
i'm so sorry i didn't give you the opportunity.

Jessica Burgos

i should have communicated my feelings to you
without covering up my pain with humor
because it is so easy to do.
when the world is burning
i can make fun of how ugly i look in the ashes
since laughter feels like healing
and it's what we do normally,
my feelings never rise to the surface
and i don't have to hear about them till they are
relevant.

i led you on to believe that i was going to
change,
that i was going to be better.

i never did
and i left you disappointed in the end.

no matter how hard i try,
no matter how much i apologize,
i can't make up for the pain i caused,
or the time that we lost.

i wish i could have been a better man to you
but i need to be a better man for me first.

Jessica Burgos

we talked about our parents and how we never
wanted to become them
but we ended up becoming
the embodiment of all their flaws.

it trickles down when
all i wanted from my father was support
in the same way he held heavy expectations for
me.
it trickles down when
all i wanted from my father was kindness
in the same way he used his voice to break me
down.
it trickles down when
my father didn't show me love,
and now i don't know how to show love either.

Jessica Burgos

i am still coping with the idea
that i have butterflies
eating at my core,
a core i never knew existed.

i am still coping with the idea
that my masculinity doesn't stop at my
physique
but that my human nature expands beneath the
seas of an adam and eve story,
expanding beneath my muscles and bones
and that i am not as shallow as i appear to be,
that i am deeper than my body
and even more real in my soul.

why is my weep considered feminine
and why is feminine considered weak
when a man's fears and a man's tears
is stronger than the sea
where there are only echos of screeches
calling out for help
and help was never given but it was always
needed.

our last conversation did not give me closure,
it only made me want more of you
so the distance between us is best
so that i hold onto me more
and hold onto you less.

i reflect on what i have learned from you:

i should be more vulnerable
or at least try to be.
i should express and verbalize my
emotions in a healthy way,
i'm so sorry that i never did.
i should learn to love my body
just as much as i love yours.
i should address my insecurities
and not make them yours.
and now, i should find closure in the way i
loved and hurt and learned.

and after we're gone
the stars will see hundreds more of me
and hundreds more of you too.

Jessica Burgos

the autumn breeze pushed us together
and now the summer breeze is pulling us apart.

and as our autumn love comes to an end,
you still keep my sweater,
and i keep your text messages like love letters,
and i leave your coffee mug on my dresser,
holding onto the memories that used to be
and i don't clean them out of my room until
months later.

we left each other in June,
and now i let the birds carry me away from
you.

you were the right woman.
not meant to be my forever, but the woman that
was meant to change me forever.

i can't erase you
or leave the memories behind
or kiss them goodbye
but when they come by,
i revisit them with kindness
and embrace them with open arms.

this year i have hit my lowest point.
i can't wait to see my what my highest looks
like.

taking a walk down memory lane
and i find the hand holding, the smoky cars and
the kiss in the fog, the small moments with you
that i used to love,
and i feel neutral.
i miss it but it's a feeling that's so subtle.
i miss you but not like i used to.

i wish you better,
i wish you the best,
because it's what you deserve

and i hope i find that too.

Jessica Burgos

and if we cross paths again,
i hope to see you happy,

even happier than you were with me.

About the Author

Jessica Burgos first became a self-published Author at sixteen years old with her poetry book, *The Art of My Color*. Her work addresses various aspects of relationships, including the love, breakup, and heartache of it all. *Finding Closure* is her second book, self-published at only twenty years old. Jessica writes based on her life experiences, which many people can relate, but cannot put into words. She finds that her purpose is inspiring people and making a space where their emotions can be comforted. Jessica is currently residing in Charlotte, North Carolina.

Printed in Great Britain
by Amazon